Scuba Steve

Marcy Schaaf

"Join Scuba Steve, the fearless underwater explorer, on a thrilling sea adventure that will take young readers on a journey beneath the waves! Dive into a world of colorful coral reefs, playful dolphins, and hidden treasures as Scuba Steve encounters friendly sea creatures and overcomes challenges in the deep blue sea. This delightful and educational storybook, perfect for children aged 5 to 8, combines fun rhymes and captivating illustrations to inspire young minds to discover the wonders of the ocean and the importance of courage and friendship."

Scuba Steve
Marcy Schaaf

This book belongs to:

In a world under the sea, lived Scuba Steve so free, With a mask on his face and fins on his feet, you see.

He swam with dolphins, oh so neat,
Through coral gardens, his heart
would beat.

Scuba Steve explored, both near and far,
In the ocean's depths, like a shining star.

With a tank on his back, he'd dive deep down,
Past shipwrecks and caves, where treasures could be found.

He met a friendly octopus,
who danced with glee,
Eight arms swirling, what
a sight to see!

A school of colorful fish joined
the fun,
Under the sea, there was room
for everyone.

Scuba Steve helped a turtle caught in a net,
Freed it with care, the encounter they'd
never forget.

He spotted a seahorse, small and so sweet, Riding on seaweed, a tiny, wiggly treat.

Down in the deep, where the sunlight grows dim, Scuba Steve found a world, full of wonders within.

But one day, a storm
raged with might, Waves
crashed above, turning
day into night.

With courage and strength, our hero stayed true,

Guiding lost fish, until the skies turned blue.

At last, he emerged from the ocean's deep blue, Scuba Steve, the brave diver, with stories anew.

So remember, my friends, as
you dream each night, The
world under the sea, is a
wondrous delight.

With Scuba Steve's spirit, and heart so bold, You can explore the oceans, as your own story unfolds.

In a world under the sea, where wonders abound, Scuba Steve's tales of adventure will always astound.

So put on your flippers, your mask, and your gear, Dive into the ocean, and let go of your fear.

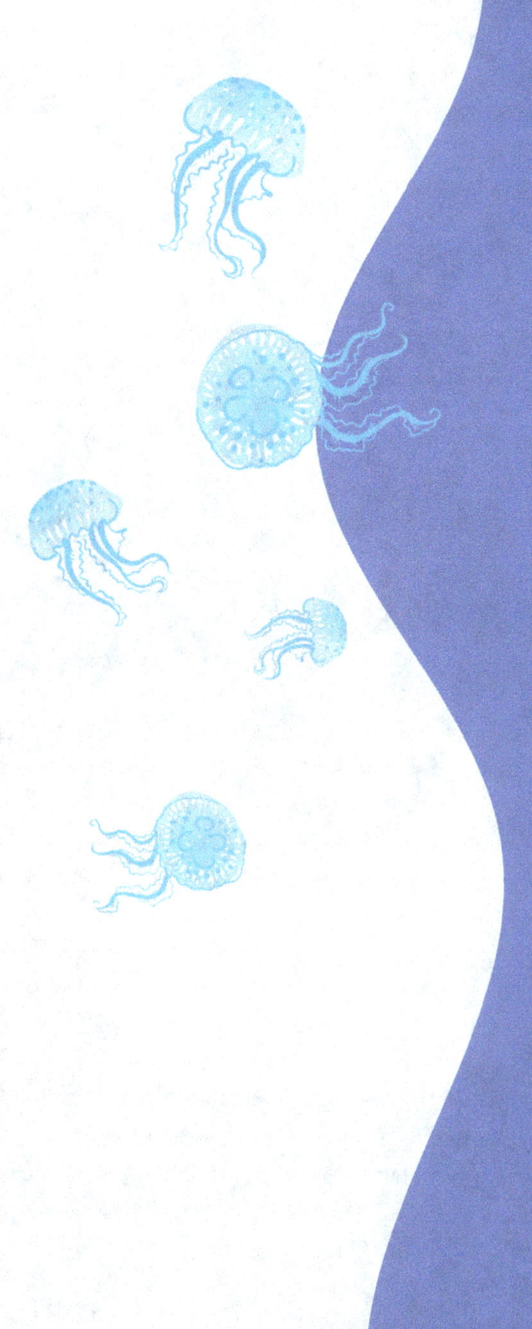

With each splash
and dive, you'll
discover anew,

The magic of the sea
, waiting just for you.

For in the deep blue, and the
ocean so vast, Adventure with
Scuba Steve will forever last.

So when you dream of the sea, as you rest in your bed, Remember Scuba Steve's adventures, and the tales that he spread.

In the world under the waves, where the mysteries reside, Scuba Steve's stories will forever be your guide.

With a heart full of wonder, and
dreams set afloat,
You can be a brave explorer, in a
scuba diver's coat.

And just like Scuba Steve, you'll find treasures untold,

In the deep, blue ocean, where your adventures unfold!

The end of our
journey, but not the
end of the fun,
For in Scuba Steve's
world, there's always
more to be done.

Thank you for
the company.

Bye!

Author Bio for Marcy Schaaf:

Marcy Schaaf is a talented writer and illustrator who has a deep passion for storytelling and the world of underwater exploration with a lifelong love for the ocean, Marcy combines her creative talents with her knowledge of marine life to bring "Scuba Steve" to life. Her enchanting illustrations and engaging narratives aim to inspire young readers to appreciate the beauty of our oceans and the importance of environmental conservation. Marcy's works invite children on exciting journeys into the depths of the sea, fostering a sense of wonder and curiosity about the natural world. She hopes her stories will encourage a new generation to become stewards of the oceans, just like Scuba Steve.

Whats your favorite fish or
is it the turtle?

What did you see at the beach?

Who do you like swimming with?

Books By Schaaf

www.BookBySchaaf.com

Find us at: